MISSION COLLEGE
LEARNING RESOURCE SERVICE

9.95

MANAGING NEGATIVE PEOPLE
Strategies for Success

S. Michael Kravitz, Ph.D.

A FIFTY-MINUTE™ SERIES BOOK

CRISP PUBLICATIONS, INC.
Menlo Park, California

3 1215 00089 7212

MANAGING NEGATIVE PEOPLE
Strategies for Success

S. Michael Kravitz, Ph.D.

STEP Process is a registered trademark of Schubert-Kravitz Associates.

CREDITS
Managing Editor: **Kathleen Barcos**
Editor: **Janis Paris**
Typesetting: **ExecuStaff**
Cover Design: **Carol Harris**
Artwork: **Ralph Mapson**

All rights reserved. No part of this book may be reproduced or transmitted in any form or by any means now known or to be invented, electronic or mechanical, including photocopying, recording, or by any information storage or retrieval system without written permission from the author or publisher, except for the brief inclusion of quotations in a review.

Copyright © 1995 Crisp Publications, Inc.
Printed in the United States of America.

English language Crisp books are distributed worldwide. Our major international distributors include:

CANADA: Reid Publishing Ltd., Box 69559—109 Thomas St., Oakville, Ontario, Canada L6J 7R4. TEL: (905) 842-4428, FAX: (905) 842-9327

Raincoast Books Distribution Ltd., 112 East 3rd Avenue, Vancouver, British Columbia, Canada V5T 1C8. TEL: (604) 873-6581, FAX: (604) 874-2711

AUSTRALIA: Career Builders, P.O. Box 1051, Springwood, Brisbane, Queensland, Australia 4127. TEL: 841-1061, FAX: 841-1580

NEW ZEALAND: Career Builders, P.O. Box 571, Manurewa, Auckland, New Zealand. TEL: 266-5276, FAX: 266-4152

JAPAN: Phoenix Associates Co., Mizuho Bldg. 2-12-2, Kami Osaki, Shinagawa-Ku, Tokyo 141, Japan. TEL: 3-443-7231, FAX: 3-443-7640

Selected Crisp titles are also available in other languages. Contact International Rights Manager Suzanne Kelly at (415) 323-6100 for more information.

Library of Congress Catalog Card Number 94-68198
Kravitz, S. Michael
Managing Negative People
ISBN 1-56052-306-9

This book is printed on recyclable paper with soy ink.

ABOUT THIS BOOK

Managing Negative People is not like most books. It has a unique "self-paced" format that encourages a reader to become personally involved. Designed to be "read with a pencil," there are exercises, activities, assessments and cases that invite participation.

Learn how to stamp out your own internal patterns of negative thinking, and overcome negativity imposed on you by others. This book includes an understanding of negative people, as well as techniques for dealing with negativity. By using the book's practical, easy-to-learn techniques, such as learning from your experience, achieving your goals, and using positive thinking, you will be able to recognize and confront negativity at work and in other areas of your life.

Managing Negative People can be used effectively in a number of ways. Here are some possibilities:

—**Individual Study.** Because the book is self-instructional, all that you need is a quiet place, some time and a pencil. Completing the activities and exercises will provide valuable feedback, as well as practical ideas for overcoming negativity in yourself and others.

—**Workshops and Seminars.** This book is ideal for use during, or as preassigned reading prior to, a workshop or seminar. With the basics in hand, the quality of participation will improve. More time can be spent practicing concept extensions and applications during the program.

—**College Programs.** Thanks to the format, brevity and low cost, this book is ideal for short courses and extension programs.

There are other possibilities that depend on the objectives of the user. One thing is certain: even after it has been read, this book will serve as excellent reference material that can easily be reviewed.

PREFACE

If you are like most people, you are confronted by negative people every day. You may even experience negative thoughts and display negative behaviors yourself. How many of you are prepared to handle so much destructiveness? Without some help or guidance to overcome negativity, you may find you have little or no joy in life at home, work or at play.

Research has clearly established that negativity leads to increased stress and conflict. A pattern of chronic stress often results in increased physical and/ or mental health problems that have an adverse impact on work, family and friends.

The purpose of this book is twofold. First, learn how to stamp out your own internal patterns of negative thinking that undermine your self-esteem. Second, learn how to confront and overcome negativity from others. With practical, easy-to-learn techniques, this book can serve as a road map to a more productive life.

Within yourself you have the power to change your own destructive thought patterns and behaviors. You may even have the power to help others turn their lives in more productive directions. By reading this book and applying the information through the many exercises, you will be better prepared to take on the world. Good luck!

S. Michael Kravitz, Ph.D.

ABOUT THE AUTHOR

S. Michael Kravitz, Ph.D., is vice-president of Schubert-Kravitz Associates, a business devoted to inspiring people to collaborate positively through knowledge and understanding.

Dr. Kravitz is a professional speaker, trainer, consultant and educator with over 30 years of practical experience. He specializes in managing negative, difficult people. Dr. Kravitz is an active member of the National Speakers Association, the Ohio Speakers Forum, and the National Management Association.

Dr. Kravitz received a B.S. in Education and both an M.A. and Ph.D. in Psychology from Ohio State University. You can reach Dr. Kravitz at:

SCHUBERT-KRAVITZ ASSOCIATES
7729 EAGLE CREEK DRIVE
PICKERINGTON, OHIO 43147
(614) 864-5111
(800) 686-8477
FAX (614) 864-5147

ACKNOWLEDGMENTS

I would like to thank all of those people in my life who have helped me overcome my own personal negativity and negativity from others. These include my loving parents, my eighth grade teacher John Kirker, Ph.D., my former partner and friend Luther Haseley, Ph.D.; and my loving and supportive wife Susan D. Schubert who helped edit the manuscript and keep me positive.

CONTENTS

INTRODUCTION

How many times have you been in situations where you felt that other people were holding you back or pulling you down? They said things like, "You will never be able to do that!" or "Take it from me, that will never work!"

Recently my wife Susan and my son Brett went to dinner with some friends and acquaintances. One of the women asked Brett what he was taking in college. When Brett stated he was in a pre-law program, she replied with a sneer and uplifted nose, "Boy, that's *just* what we need, another lawyer!" Perceiving Brett's irritation, Susan interrupted with, "Yes, that's just what we *do* need, another *good* lawyer!"

If you let negative, critical messages like the one in this example take over and control your thinking, they can interfere with your success. It is likely you will give up and never even try.

When dealing with negative people it is extremely important to rule out physical/medical and severe psychological causes because these individuals must be dealt with in a different manner than those with learned negative patterns. Physical causes of negativity may include depression, anxiety, inadequate personality development, chronic pain, uncontrolled diabetes, some medical conditions and some medications. While the techniques described in this book will work with most negative people, they will not be as successful with conditions that are primarily physical/medical or severely psychological in nature. Until these issues are dealt with by the appropriate medical/psychological professional, environmental or behavioral changes will not have as much impact. If you consider yourself a negative person and suspect there may be physical, medical or severe psychological causes, I recommend you seek an assessment from a qualified professional.

The entire focus of this book is to give people the necessary information and practical strategies to overcome negativity and difficult people in both the workplace and other settings. Everyone has to learn how to manage negativity, whether it's internal or from others. *Managing Negative People* is a positive route to a successful future.

S E C T I O N

I

Understanding Negative People

WHY IS DEALING WITH NEGATIVITY IMPORTANT?

People with negative emotions (often related to a poor self-concept) have a much greater chance of experiencing negative stress and distress and are more likely to experience dissatisfaction with their lives and jobs. Some of the results of negativity include increased absenteeism and use of medical benefits and, in many cases, can result in lowered productivity and happiness. By learning how to cope with negativity (both from self and others), individuals are more likely to find their life and work more satisfying and productive.

A concrete example will help illustrate the financial impact of negativity on business. According to the American Management Association, approximately 65 percent of the average company's business comes from its present satisfied customers.

If an organization has negative customer service employees, these employees are likely to lose customers for the company. The loss of *one customer a day for a year* who typically spends $50 per week would cost a company nearly 1/2 million dollars a year. This is only the financial loss. What about the loss of emotional energy, self-confidence, and morale that was wasted in the process?

DO YOU KNOW WHERE NEGATIVITY COMES FROM?

WHERE DOES NEGATIVITY COME FROM?

Some people appear to be born with a genetic predisposition toward negativity, while others appear to become negative as a result of their environment. Psychologists have long argued about the basis of each individual's personality. This debate has been resolved by those who agree that one's personality is a combination of our genetic make-up and our life experiences.

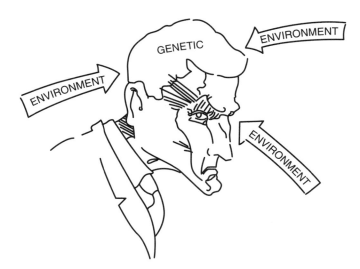

For purposes of this book, people who express negativity a majority of the time will be referred to as *Negators*. Negators are people who chronically express negative thoughts, feelings, and behaviors that increase the likelihood of engaging in destructive actions. Negativity can be experienced in two ways: 1) Imposed by others, or 2) Caused by our own thoughts and feelings.

Before you learn how to manage Negators, it is important to understand how you personally experience negativity. You can do this by completing the worksheet included here.

HOW DO YOU EXPERIENCE NEGATIVITY?

Negativity can be experienced in two ways: things you tell yourself and things others tell you. By completing this workplace survey, you can determine the sources of your internal negativity.

Survey 1: How You Experience Negativity

Directions: Please rank the four primary causes of your negativity, which may include your thoughts, feelings, and behaviors.

**Your
Ranking**   **Causes**

_____   Hurt Feelings, Being Rejected by Others

_____   Hurt Feelings, Seldom Given Support or Positive Feedback

_____   Being Taken Advantage of

_____   Not Feeling as Good About Yourself as You Would Like

_____   Work Criticized by Others

_____   Fear of Change

_____   Taking Action Too Slowly

_____   Being Forced to Lower Your Standards

_____   Being Isolated from People

_____   What You Want to Do Is in Conflict with What You Feel You
          Should Do

_____   Negativity Has Become a Habitual Pattern

HOW DO YOU EXPERIENCE NEGATIVITY? (continued)

Survey Results

How do your experiences compare to others? According to my recent survey of a cross section of over 200 employees in business, industry, education and professional associations, here are the major causes of negativity. They are listed in rank order with the most frequent cause at the top.

Your Ranking	Causes
1	Hurt Feelings, Seldom Given Support, or Positive Feedback
2	What You Want to Do Is in Conflict with What You Feel You Should Do
3	Not Feeling as Good About Yourself as You Would Like
4	Being Taken Advantage of
5	Hurt Feelings, Being Rejected by Others
6	Work Criticized by Others
7	Being Isolated from People
8	Fear of Change
9	Taking Action Too Slowly
10	Being Forced to Lower Your Standards
11	Negativity Has Become a Habitual Pattern

Of the six most common causes, four are related to personal needs, one to values, and one to self-esteem. These results indicate that needs and values, as well as self-esteem, are among the primary causes of negativity, while "habitual patterns" are the least likely causes of our negativity.

Survey 2: Your Internal Negativity

Negativity can be experienced in two ways: things you tell yourself and things others tell you. Survey 2 indicates the nature of your own internal negative thinking.

Directions: Select a work, family or social focus and rate each of the thoughts below on the following scale:

0 = rarely or never
1 = occasionally
2 = about half of the time
3 = frequently

Focus_____

_____ "I can't do it"

_____ "I'll never be able to —"

_____ "It won't do any good"

_____ "Why try?"

_____ "No one cares"

_____ "It won't work"

_____ "No one ever really thinks things through around here"

Add up your ratings and insert the total I.N. (Internal Negativity) Score below.

TOTAL I.N. SCORE:_____

HOW DO YOU EXPERIENCE NEGATIVITY? (continued)

Survey 3: Negativity from Others

By completing this survey, you will be able to determine the nature of the negativity you receive from others.

Directions: Negativity can also be generated by others. Keeping the same focus you selected in Survey 2 (FOCUS_____), rate each of the items below on the following Scale:

    0 = rarely or never
    1 = occasionally
    2 = about half of the time
    3 = frequently

One or more people:

_____ orders you around

_____ does not listen to you when you talk

_____ ignores your feelings

_____ overreacts to situations

_____ finds fault with what you do

_____ points out your mistakes

_____ is pessimistic

_____ gets even in a sneaky way (sabotages your work)

_____ intentionally forgets to follow through on your requests

_____ is slow to follow through on your requests

Add up your ratings and insert the total N.O. (Negativity from Others) Score below.

TOTAL N.O. SCORE:_____

INTERPRETATION OF NEGATIVITY WORKSHEETS

Survey 1: Interpretation

Directions: These results compare how you personally experience negativity with the survey results (a cross section sample of others). Return to Survey 1 on page 5 and write the four primary causes of your negativity adjacent to YOUR RANKING column below. Then, from the survey results given previously, place the survey ranking for your four causes under the "SURVEY RANKING" column.

How You Experience Negativity (Four Primary Causes)

Causes	Your Ranking	Survey Ranking
1._____	_____	_____
2._____	_____	_____
3._____	_____	_____
4._____	_____	_____

Survey 2: Interpretation

Directions: Refer to Survey 2 on page 7 for your total I.N. (Internal Negativity) score, and obtain your rating from the following key:

Total I.N. Score: _____

```
0–5    = low
6–10   = moderate
11–16  = high
24–30  = severe
```

INTERPRETATION OF NEGATIVITY WORKSHEETS (continued)

Survey 3: Interpretation

Directions: Refer to Survey 3 on page 8 for your total N.O. (Negativity from Others) score, and obtain your rating from the following key:

Total N.O. Score: _____

        0–7   = low
        8–15 = moderate
        16–23 = high
        17–21 = severe

More Interpretation

Insert the ratings you obtained from Surveys 2 and 3 below:

Total Internal Negativity Rating   _____

Total Negativity from Others Rating _____

My research using this survey discovered one important finding. Respondents tended to be either high or low in both internal negativity and negativity from others. While no causal relationship can be proven, the implication is that having one source of negativity increases the chances of having the other. How close were your ratings?

In my experience, there is also a relationship between the primary causes of internal negativity and an individual's effectiveness in dealing with specific types of negative people. This relationship will be discussed later.

WHAT CAUSES NEGATIVE, DIFFICULT PEOPLE?

The five major internal sources of negative, difficult behavior are: motivation by needs, motivation by values, attitudes, norms, and self-esteem. This section explains the relationship between these internal sources of negativity and people's thoughts, feelings and actions. Whatever the cause, negativity can become a habitual pattern of thinking, communicating and acting. It can become so ingrained in our lives that we fail to see the goodness in and around us.

What Is Motivation?

If we want to know why someone is negative, we can determine the answer by finding out what motivates him or her. Other peoples' motivations are unique and may differ from ours. Two types of drives motivate us: needs and values. "Needs motivation" includes our needs for such things as security, love and growth. "Values motivation" is the principles or beliefs we have learned and developed over a lifetime. Values are the "oughts" and "shoulds" of life.

WHAT CAUSES NEGATIVE, DIFFICULT PEOPLE? (continued)

Needs Motivation

Motivation is why people do what they do. In the 1960s, the psychologist Abraham Maslow first described levels of needs. The most basic needs are survival and security. Once these needs are met, nurturance needs (belonging and love) are at the second level. When the first two need levels are satisfied, individuals seek opportunities to grow, develop and achieve in their lives. Individuals who are functioning primarily at the survival level tend to be negative, while those operating at the growth level are more likely to be positively oriented.

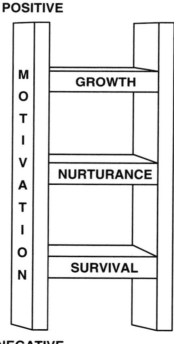

Needs Motivation Assessment

Finding out what motivates people is not an easy process. A useful starting point is asking people what motivates them. Once information about causes has been gathered, you can use an organized system to help determine, clarify and understand others' and your own motivational systems. As noted already, two of the motivational aspects of negative, difficult behavior are that these people are driven by needs and values.

Needs Driven Motivation—The organized needs driven system utilized in this book is called the STEP System™. Based on an analysis of a negative person's unique style, the STEP System™ provides corresponding coping techniques. To determine what needs drive your behavior, complete the assessment on the next page.

THE STEP SYSTEM™ TO BETTER COMMUNICATION

By understanding what motivates you and others to do what you do in specific situations, your communications and interactions with others can be improved. In other words, to improve your communications with others, watch your step. (Please note: the STEP System™ is only an introduction to the concept of communication or behavior styles.)

Name: _____ Date: _____

Specific Situation: _____

Assessment Directions: When interacting with others in a specific situation involving negativity from others, I am best described by the following words (please circle all that apply, ignoring the word "motivates").

S	T	E	P
Stable	Thorough	Emotional	Pusher
Systematic	Questioning	Outgoing	Assertive
Cooperative	Analytical	Happy	Aggressive
Specialist	Perfectionist	Likes People	In Control
Reserved	Unemotional	Talkative	Quick
Security	Organized	Being Liked	Results-Oriented
motivates	motivates	motivates	motivates
_____	_____	_____	_____

Once you have finished circling the above words, total the number of words circled in each one of the four columns. The rest of the scoring and interpretation is continued on the next page.

Adapted from "Personal Profile System,"® Carlson Learning Company. See References in the back of the book for more information.

Interpretation

Select the one or two columns with the highest number of words circled. The first word at the top of each column describes your communications or behavior style. For example, if the most circled words are in the third column, your behavior style is Emotional. The last word (above motivates) in each column describes the motivation for that style.

My style(s) is best described as (insert the top word in selected column or columns). _____

My style is motivated by my need for (insert last word in selected column or columns). _____

Before we go any further, it is important to note that we are a blend of all four of these styles, but we tend to exhibit some more than others. In order to more clearly illustrate each of the four styles, let us assume each of these is separate and distinct.

The results of this assessment also provide you with an additional understanding about yourself and others. As previously explained, the STEP System™ helps you understand why people are driven to do what they do; in other words, their needs motivate their behavior. This system is like a road map. Maps help you understand where you are and how to get somewhere else. In the same way, the STEP System™ helps you to better understand current relationships with others, and how to get from where you are to where you want to be.

In line with the map analogy, there are no right or wrong directions, only those which will help us get to where we are going and those which will not. In the same way, there are no right or wrong styles. However, some styles are more likely to result in conflict in certain situations or with other specific styles. For example, if there is a fire and your natural style is to talk with everyone about what you should do, you are likely to get burned! Your natural style is not effective in this situation. To be truly successful in life, the ability and willingness to adapt to the needs of other people and situations is necessary. In their book *People Smart*, Michael O'Connor and Tony and Janice Allesandra refer to this as the Platinum Rule.

> *Platinum Rule:* "Treat other people the way they need to be treated."

THE STEP SYSTEM™ TO BETTER COMMUNICATION (continued)

Each one of the four styles in the STEP System™ can be expressed positively or negatively. While the Platinum Rule is important for dealing with positively expressed styles, it is absolutely necessary for dealing more effectively with Negators.

Since you must understand the STEP System™ before dealing with the negative expressions of each style, a summary description of each style and its related motivators is provided below.

Matching Styles to Motivators

COMMUNICATION STYLE	MOTIVATORS
STABLE	
Specialists, systematic, reserved, stable, cooperative	Feeling secure, liking team work
THOROUGH	
Perfectionists, organized, analytical, questioning, unemotional	Doing things exactly the right way
EMOTIONAL	
Happy, talkative, outgoing, likes people, being liked	Enjoying that people like them, having fun
PUSHER	
In control, quick, assertive, results-oriented, aggressive	Getting things done fast, being in control

Exercise: Define the Style

Read each of the following statements and indicate which style is involved.

1. "John, get this done right now! I don't have time to talk about it, just do it!"

   Style _____

2. "Mary, I would appreciate knowing ahead of time when you would like to have things done. Also, I can do a better job for you if you tell me how you want me to do something. A system I can use over and over would really be helpful for me. That way our team can work better together."

   Style _____

3. "I really like it when we all go out for lunch together. It's always so much fun, almost like a party! We can talk with each other and get caught up on what's happening."

   Style _____

4. "I am most productive when I can do quality work. For example, I really did a good job developing our policy and procedure manual. It took a long time, but my thorough analysis resulted in a precise, detailed manual. Some people even told me I was a perfectionist. I took that as a compliment."

   Style _____

5. "I can't stand it when we run out of pencils! This just shouldn't happen. You know it's not my fault! It really makes me feel like people don't like me! I can't have fun when stuff like this happens."

   Style _____

THE STEP SYSTEM™ TO BETTER COMMUNICATION (continued)

6. "When I don't know what's going to happen, I can't organize my schedule the right way. Why don't they tell me ahead of time? If I know, I can plan and prepare for the things that are likely to go wrong. That way they won't happen, even though something else probably will."

Style _____

7. "He never listens to me or tells me how to do things. I really like to work as part of a team, but I don't know how to do this project and he's gone for the day. I've had enough of this. I'll do this project for him, but I'll do it the way I did the last project even though this is entirely different. It's a system that I'm familiar with. It probably won't be done the way he wants, but he never took the time to tell me, and there is no one else here who can help."

Style _____

8. "I've worked here for 30 years and I'm telling you this is the way to do it! If you want to get results around here just do it this way and stop arguing with me! I don't have time for this!"

Style _____

Interpretation

Did you have any trouble? The correct answers are 1) Pusher, 2) Stable, 3) Emotional, 4) Thorough, 5) Emotional, 6) Thorough, 7) Stable, and 8) Pusher. Each of the four communication or behavior styles was represented twice; the first time in a more positive manner (1 to 4), while the second time in a more negative way (5 to 8). Dealing with these negative expressions will be the focus of the next section of this book.

OTHER CAUSES OF NEGATIVE, DIFFICULT PEOPLE

VALUES-DRIVEN MOTIVATION

Values are the "oughts" and "shoulds" of life, the guideposts by which you make decisions. Everyone is motivated by needs, but sometimes values can come into conflict with needs. To illustrate a conflict between needs and values, consider a woman who places great value on higher education. She finds herself working on a course paper at 1:00 A.M. on the day on which it is due. Because she values dependability, she feels compelled to complete the paper. However, there is a physical need for sleep. Does the paper get finished? It all depends on which motivation is stronger at the time.

SELF-ESTEEM

The level of your self-esteem or how good you feel about yourself is one of the main factors in determining how people choose to react to a situation or event. This is illustrated in the Self-Esteem Model given here. At the top of the model, people who feel good about themselves and their activities tend to see new situations as opportunities and challenges. They are often eager and excited about the opportunity provided by the situation.

On the lower level of the model, those who have had few successes and view themselves as failures (they lack self-esteem) tend to feel threatened and fearful, resulting in defensive or angry behavior. The destructive results continue to reinforce feelings of being threatened and negative thinking. This sets up a pattern of self-destructive behavior. Obviously, something must be done to stop this process. Some techniques for doing so will be described later in this book.

OTHER CAUSES OF NEGATIVE, DIFFICULT PEOPLE (continued)

SELF-ESTEEM MODEL

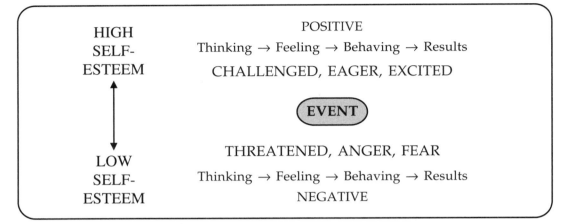

The same event or situation elicits a different reaction from a person in the high and positive level versus someone at the low and negative level. Generally, a good self-concept leads to positive thinking and a person is likely to feel eager and excited when given a challenge. A person with a poor self-concept is more likely to have negative thinking and feelings and respond with angry, fearful behaviors to many situations, which they perceive as threatening.

(ATTITUDES)

Webster's New World Dictionary defines attitude as "A way of acting, feeling or thinking; one's disposition, mental set." In a sense, attitudes are filters through which we view the world. Negative attitudes prevent us and others from getting what we want in our lives. Negative thinking and feeling often lead to negative actions. Our life experiences and level of self-esteem help determine our attitudes.

Self-Esteem and Attitudes

Often individuals with poor self-esteem also have negative attitudes about themselves, others, and the world in general. Those with negative attitudes tend to distort reality and see the world as a place where everyone is going to get in their way. A better knowledge of your current level of self-esteem and your attitudes should help you deal more effectively with negativity. You can determine these levels by completing the following Self-Esteem and Attitude Assessment.

Self-Esteem and Attitude Assessment

Directions: Rate yourself on a four-point scale for each one of the following statements.

> 3 = always
> 2 = over half of the time
> 1 = occasionally
> 0 = never

_____ 1. When someone compliments me, I do not have any difficulty accepting the compliment.

_____ 2. When I meet a person for the first time, I see their positive qualities first.

_____ 3. I feel good about myself and my competencies.

_____ 4. When confronted by a new situation, I view it as an opportunity or challenge.

_____ 5. I can close my eyes and see myself accomplishing my goals.

_____ 6. When confronted with a problem, I engage in positive thinking and/or planning.

_____ 7. If asked, people would describe me as a positive person.

_____ 8. I develop plans and work toward my goals.

_____ 9. I believe my actions have a great deal to do with my happiness/success in life.

_____ TOTAL POINTS

The results are interpreted on the next page.

OTHER CAUSES OF NEGATIVE, DIFFICULT PEOPLE (continued)

Assessment Interpretation

23–27 Points = Great self-esteem. You feel good about yourself and your capabilities. You are an optimist with positive attitudes.

18–22 Points = Good self-esteem. Usually, you feel good about yourself and your capabilities. Overall, you are an optimist with positive attitudes.

14–17 Points = Moderate self-esteem. There are times when you experience self-doubts. You vary between being an optimist and a pessimist, although you tend to be more positive than negative.

9–13 Points = Diminished self-esteem. There are times when you experience self-doubts. You vary between being an optimist and a pessimist, although you tend to be more negative than positive.

0–8 Points = Negative self-esteem. You do not feel good about yourself and your capabilities. You are a pessimist who usually has negative attitudes.

(NORMS)

The last major cause of negativity is related to what are referred to as norms or standards of conduct that are typical for a specific group. For example, if you were raised in a family environment where everyone else was negative, you will tend to be negative. Negativity can become habitual, normal behavior for a family that is negative most of the time.

Summary

There are many causes of negative behavior. Our needs and values can motivate negative behavior, as well as our level of self-esteem, attitudes, and norms. The remainder of this book will focus on practical interventions and changes that will help the reader who wants to obtain success and personal fulfillment overcome negative people.

Now that you have a better understanding of negative people, the next section will help you remember specific actions you can take when communicating with Negators.

SECTION

II

Dealing with Negativity

DEALING WITH OTHERS' NEGATIVITY

In order to deal effectively with Negators, this part of the book provides five essential skills for dealing with others' negativity. These skills will help you master your own emotions and communications. Master these skills before moving on to later sections.

SKILL #1: Avoid Personalizing

Remember the focus of this book is on people who are chronically negative. Negators are negative with everyone, not just you. You need to tell yourself repeatedly that it is irrational to take anything they say personally. By avoiding defensiveness and overreactions you will remain in control. When you are in control of your own emotions, you can confront Negators in a positive, constructive manner by successfully using some of the techniques described in this book.

As indicated in the Self-Esteem Model in the previous section, individuals who do not feel good about themselves tend to perceive the world in a negative manner. Their negativity is usually intensified when they are around other Negators. For this reason the number of chronically negative people in your life should be minimized until you master some of this book's techniques.

SKILL #2: Use "I" Messages

A technique that will help you cope with some Negators is to replace the pronoun "you" with the pronoun "I." How have you reacted to someone who said the following:

> "How could *you* do that?"
>
> "What is wrong with *you*?"
>
> "Why are *you* speeding?"

People in general, but especially negative people, tend to get upset when they get "you'd" out. "I" statements are much more acceptable and less likely to upset others. Replace "Why are *you* speeding?" with "*I* get upset and anxious when people speed." This approach tends to work best when you are dealing with loved ones or with your own personal negative thoughts.

DEALING WITH OTHERS' NEGATIVITY (continued)

SKILL #3: Deal with Their Anger

Negators are often angry. In order to remain in positive control follow these directions:

1. Breathe.

2. Speak.

3. Process.

These approaches will not only help keep you relaxed and in control, they also will help reduce the anger in others.

Breathe Slowly and Regularly

Slow down your breathing rate. You can easily do this by breathing in and out as slowly as you can (count from 1 to 8, hold your breath for several seconds before exhaling, and then slowly count from 8 to 1). When you do this for a few minutes, you and your body begin to relax. Your heart and breathing rates decrease while you reduce any sweating or flushing that has occurred. By remaining as relaxed as possible you are in a better position to think about what you are going to do next to maintain positive control of the situation.

Repeat this process ten times if necessary. With some practice you can easily use this technique when confronted by angry Negators.

Speak in a Calm Manner

You can both slow down the rate and lower the volume of your speech. Both of these techniques have a calming effect on angry Negators; at the same time they help you relax and retain or regain control. Imagine yourself confronting someone who is angry and upset with you. If you raise your voice and speak rapidly, what do you think will happen? The opposite is usually true if you slow down and reduce the volume of your speech.

USE THE *UAR* PROCESS

In addition to the specific techniques described above, following the UAR process can help you reduce anger from others. While this process will not work well with those who are totally irrational, it works well with many angry Negators.

UNDERSTAND: LISTEN AND PROVIDE FEEDBACK

Angry negators need to be heard. It is extremely important to let angry people vent their feelings. You can do so by listening. Focus on what the other person is trying to convey. When necessary ask a question to help clarify understanding, but let them do most of the talking. Then give feedback or summarize your perception of what they said to let them know you have an accurate understanding of their concerns.

APOLOGIZE: BLAMELESSLY

Most angry people are sensitive and their feelings are easily hurt. For this reason an apology is helpful. However, the apology should be blameless in order to prevent a new focus for the negativity or the anger. For example, don't say "I'm sorry the production department has ignored your request." Instead, say "I'm sorry. I know how frustrating it is when things like this happen." This will help both you and the Negator focus on solving the problem rather than dwelling on who might be at fault.

RESOLVE: SPECIFY ACTIONS

What are you going to do to resolve the problem? Tell the person what you are going to do and when you are going to do it. Make certain you include specific timelines and an easy way for them to contact you if necessary. Since angry people are not as rational as when they are calm, it is often beneficial to help them outline what actions they have agreed to take.

USE THE *UAR* PROCESS (continued)

Deal with Their Anger

The following example illustrates this process.

UAR Case Example

Ms. Jones has reached me by telephone with the following conversation: "You know I'm really upset with all of this. I called your office this morning and then two more times, once just before lunch and once just after lunch. No one has bothered to call me back. What's wrong over there?"

UNDERSTAND: Listen to the angry individual and only ask questions to clarify. This is followed by feedback. "Then what you are upset about is having called three times and no one returned your call?" If this person indicates this is an accurate statement, then you move on to the next step. Otherwise, ask another question or two in order to ensure accurate understanding.

APOLOGIZE: "Ms. Jones, I apologize for your calls not being returned. We are really concerned about your inconvenience." (Do not blame yourself, them or someone else.)

RESOLVE: "I am going to find out why your calls were not returned so you or any other customers will not be inconvenienced like this again. I will call you back with an explanation at 3:00 P.M. this afternoon if that is convenient. If that's OK, would you like me to transfer you now to someone who can take care of your merchandise return? If you have any other problems, please feel free to call me between 9 and 5 weekdays."

In order to practice this process complete the UAR Worksheet that follows. First, describe a situation in the last six months in which you had to deal with someone who was angry. Then write what you could say or do for each of the UAR sections.

```
┌─────────────────────────────────────────────────────────┐
│                    UAR Worksheet                          │
│                                                           │
│  Situation:_____  │
│           _____  │
│           _____  │
│                                                           │
│  Understand:_____  │
│             _____  │
│             _____  │
│                                                           │
│  Apologize:_____  │
│            _____  │
│            _____  │
│                                                           │
│  Resolve:_____  │
│          _____  │
│          _____  │
└─────────────────────────────────────────────────────────┘
```

Remove Yourself from Irrational People

After you have used specific techniques and the UAR process without successfully alleviating the Negator's anger, it is necessary to remove yourself from the situation. Ask yourself the following question to determine if the other person is irrational: "Is there *anything* that I can say or do that will make this person feel any better?" If the answer is "no" you must temporarily leave the situation. This action allows time for the anger to dissipate to the point where logic can be used to resolve the problem. If this action is not taken you run the risk of losing control at the very time when the other person has already done so. When both parties lose control, they express anger in a highly destructive manner, often resulting in loss of a personal relationship or a customer.

USE THE *UAR* PROCESS (continued)

Before removing yourself from the situation, make certain you lay the ground work for a future session, usually within several hours to one day. Obviously, it is important to keep this future appointment. In some cases you may want to include a third party such as your supervisor to help resolve the problem. If so, make sure the angry party knows your intentions in advance. Again, avoid using the pronoun "you." Here is an example of how you might phrase this:

We are too upset to talk about this now. I would like to set up another time to talk this afternoon. What time is better for you, 3:00 P.M., 6:00 P.M. or another time? I think it could be helpful to have ____ present to help us resolve this problem.

SKILL #4: Confront Negative Conflict

Negators can be particularly difficult to deal with in conflict situations. In addition to the UAR process, the following guidelines will help you deal with the conflict:

► **Focus on the Issues, Not Personalities**

Say "We are here to deal with . . . , not to find someone to blame." Avoid thinking, saying, or doing anything that might devalue a person or make someone feel bad. If you are too upset to talk with the Negator, you should reschedule the meeting.

► **Understand Their Feelings**

Put yourself in others' shoes by attempting to see things from their viewpoint. Consider what's important to them, what they have to gain or lose in the conflict.

► **Express Your Ideas and Feelings**

Make every effort to express yourself in a positive, constructive manner. Again, use "I" messages. For example, "I feel unsure of what to do next. I really want to work this out."

► **Be Willing to Compromise**

After listening with an open mind, be willing to modify your position based on the other person's input. However, make certain the new position is one you feel is fair and equitable.

SKILL #5: Turn Things Around

How many times have Negators complained to you about why things will not work? They can give you dozens of reasons why something will not succeed. Negators are also skilled at using sarcasm to destroy people and their ideas. A great deal of their and your emotional energy goes into these negative communications. By turning things around you can divert this negativity into positive, constructive efforts. Two techniques especially useful for turning things around are 1) Asking what can be done and 2) Using *opposite statements*.

Using Opposite Statements

The use of this technique was explained in the introduction when my wife Susan and my son Brett went out to dinner with some friends. When one of the women stated "Boy, that's just what we need, *another* lawyer," Susan's reply was "Yes, that's what we *do* need, another *good* lawyer." She confronted this negativity by turning the situation around with her opposite statement. This technique can also be used by repeating or exaggerating the Negator's statement.

Example:

NEGATOR: "You never do what I want to do."

YOU: "I **never** do what you want to do?"

or

NEGATOR: "If my boss gets on my case one more time, I'm going to punch his lights out."

YOU: "You're going to do **what** to your boss?"

Asking What Can Be Done

After you have listened to a Negator list numerous reasons why something will not work, simply ask them for positive, constructive suggestions for what can be done to help make it work. It is often helpful to tell the Negator not to talk with you again until they have some constructive suggestions.

WHEN YOU ARE THE NEGATIVE PERSON

Up to this point in the book, you have primarily studied ways to manage others' negativity. One's own personal negativity can be even more challenging to overcome. Following is a worksheet to begin this process. You will have an opportunity to complete it at the end of this book.

Describe the problem in behavioral terms. What would it look like on videotape? _____

_____

_____

What are your negative thoughts? _____

_____

_____

From the five possible causes of negativity (needs, values, self-esteem, attitudes and norms), list what you think are the primary causes of your negativity. _____

_____

_____

What is your behavioral or communication style(s)? _____

_____

_____

What motivates you? _____

_____

_____

What are the best strategies for dealing with your own negative messages?

_____

_____

Is your self-esteem below average? If it is, what can be done to help you increase it? _____

_____

_____

SECTION

III

Understanding Negators' Styles

NEGATOR STYLES

As you have learned in the discussion of the STEP System™, there are four different behavioral or communication styles that help us understand what motivates people to do what they do. Each of these styles can be expressed in both positive and negative terms.

The following chart summarizes the relationship between the positive and negative sides of the STEP System™.

	Positive Expression	Negative Expression	Motivation
STABLE	Cooperative, a team player	Passive-resistant, back-stabbing	Security
THOROUGH	Precise, accurate, organized	Nit-picker, cynical	Doing things the right way
EMOTIONAL	Outgoing, friendly, verbal	Overly dramatic, exaggerates	Approval, having fun
PUSHER	Initiates action, gets results	Aggressive-teller, demanding	Wants quick results, control

Cooperation is the key!

I value accuracy!

We'll go further with friendliness!

I want results . . . now!

Identifying Negator Styles

You must carefully observe a negator before you plan to confront him or her. If possible, try to match their observable behavior to the behaviors described in the STEP System™. You must carefully listen to how and why they communicate for clues about what motivates them. If you have a good relationship, you may ask what motivates or is important to them.

In order to help you apply the STEP approach, familiarize yourself with examples of negative styles. You can do this by completing the following quiz.

NEGATOR STYLE QUIZ

Directions: After reading each one of the following statements, write in the behavior style that best matches the negative behavior. Please choose from the following Negator styles:

Stable	**Thorough**	**Emotional**	**Pusher**
Passive-Resistant	Cynical, Nit-Picker	Overly Dramatic	Aggressive-Teller

1. You asked Tomas, a fellow employee, for a report at 9:00 A.M. Tomas has had several conflicts with you in the past. It is now 3:00 P.M. and after you have asked for the report two more times he still has not done it. When asked the fourth time he replies, "Oh, I keep forgetting to do it."

What is Tomas' style? _____

2. "I told you to get this project turned in; get it done now!"

What style did this person use? _____

3. "If you prepare for something that is likely to go wrong, it won't happen, but something else will! If you don't go over everything and check it for accuracy, all kinds of mistakes are made."

This person's style is _____

4. "You forgot to order pencils! Our boss won't like us and everyone else will complain we didn't do our part. This is just terrible, another thing that will be held against us. This is just about the worst thing that's ever happened!"

What is the style of the speaker? _____

5. You asked Martha to review a project proposal before it is submitted to your boss. Martha returned two days later and gave you the following feedback. "You know this proposal isn't done right. Although it's listed in the procedures manual, I would never use it because new people are likely to make more errors. Also you made your margins one-and-a-half inches wide. If you do that you will have to use more paper, and that's a waste."

What is Martha's style? _____

6. John has had three 5-minute social conversations at break. As he walks back to his work area he attempts to socialize with Shana, who says she is too busy to talk right now. John thinks to himself "I just don't know what to do around here. I can't make everyone like me. Every time I try to socialize, the other employees don't talk to me. It's really no fun to work here anymore!"

What is John's style? _____

7. "If you want to succeed around here you need to do it my way! You should do it this way. I already told you once not to do it that way! Do it!"

What is this person's style? _____

8. An employee is very upset and angry with his boss. As he sits at his desk and works, he is thinking, "I'll get even with him. I'll just put this proposal for review in an inner-office mail envelope and keep it in my private files until it's past due. Then, I'll drop it in the office mail box when no one is looking. Boy, that will sure get him in trouble!"

What is his style? _____

IDENTIFYING NEGATOR STYLES
(continued)

Interpretation

How well did you do? The correct answers and the reasons why are:

1. **Stable (Passive-Resistant)** Tomas is passively telling his work associate he does not want to cooperate with him. He has trouble dealing directly with conflict.

2. **Pusher (Aggressive-Teller)** Quick results are demanded.

3. **Thorough (Cynical, Nit-Picker)** This is a cynical statement; the person also worries about accuracy.

4. **Emotional (Overly Dramatic)** This person is overreacting to the situation and feels other people won't like her.

5. **Thorough (Cynical, Nit-Picker)** There is concern for doing it the right way, and the nature of the interaction is cynical.

6. **Emotional (Overly Dramatic)** He overreacts to feeling rejected by others.

7. **Pusher (Aggressive-Teller)** She is aggressively telling you to do something, and she obviously wants to control the situation to get results.

8. **Stable (Passive-Resistant)** This employee's expression of resentment/anger is being done in a sneaky, non-confrontational way.

The Most Difficult Negator Styles

Everyone has certain negators who are more difficult to deal with than others. This is largely due to our personal, natural communication style. The next chart indicates these tendencies.

Personal Style and Ability to Deal with Negators

This table indicates the four communication/behavior styles and the specific Negator styles that are usually the most difficult to deal with for each style. If you have identified your primary style, the "Degree of Difficulty" column indicates the communication styles you will find the most challenging.

Communication Challenges

Your Style	Degree of Difficulty	
	Most Difficulty	*Some Difficulty*
STABLE	aggressive-teller	overly dramatic
THOROUGH	aggressive-teller	overly dramatic
EMOTIONAL	cynic, nit-picker	passive-resistant
PUSHER	cynic, nit-picker	passive-resistant

While the above is usually true, there are exceptions. When dealing with a Negator that has a similar style, there can be two outcomes. If you have not yet learned how to overcome the negativity from yourself and others, you are likely to have difficulty dealing with someone with the same style. On the other hand, if you have been personally successful in overcoming negativity, you are more likely to deal well with someone with a similar style.

MATCHING COMMUNICATION STRATEGIES

These communication strategies generally work well with each of the four styles, but are especially important when working with Negators. When confronted by negative styles, find the corresponding matching strategies from the following lists.

Matching Strategies

STABLE	THOROUGH	EMOTIONAL	PUSHER
security, cooperation	*right way, precision*	*being liked, fun*	*control, results*
Listen and Support	Be Prepared and Organized	Let Them Talk	Yield Control
Give Feedback	Be Precise and Accurate	Be Friendly and Supportive	Be Brief
Provide Guidelines	Provide Positive Feedback	Listen to Their Concerns	Focus on Business
Reduce Risks	Allow Time for Decisions	Avoid Too Much Detail	Summarize Research
Prepare for Change	Support Arguments with Logic	Provide Time for Fun	Appeal to Quick Results
Recognize Their Efforts	Help Set More Reasonable Expectations	Appeal to Their Being Liked	Let Them Make Decisions
Encourage Expression of Their Feelings			

Exercise: Apply What You Have Learned

1. Identify a situation that appears to cause you to be negative (internal messages), or identify a Negator with whom you frequently have to deal on a regular basis. (Remember, with individuals and situations where the primary causes of negativity are physical/medical or severely psychological in nature, the greater the difficulty in dealing with them unless other outside medical and/or psychological interventions are involved.)

_____

_____

_____

2. How do you experience this negativity?

_____

_____

_____

3. From the five possible causes of negativity (needs, values, attitudes, norms, and self-esteem), list what you think are the primary causes of negativity for this Negator or for yourself.

_____

_____

_____

4. Select any of the techniques mentioned earlier that you feel would be helpful in confronting the negativity in question. Most of these techniques will not apply to your own negative messages, but primarily for dealing with Negators.

_____

_____

_____

MATCHING COMMUNICATION STRATEGIES (continued)

5. Identify either your behavioral style or that of the Negator (Stable, Thorough, Emotional, Pusher) and what motivates that style.

_____

_____

_____

6. Write down the best communication or other strategies for dealing with the Negator in question or for dealing with your own negative messages.

_____

_____

_____

7. Is the level of self-esteem below average? If so what can be done to increase it?

_____

_____

_____

8. What, if anything, can be done to reduce perceived threat?

_____

_____

_____

9. What can be done to make the situation more challenging?

_____

_____

_____

S E C T I O N

IV

Overcoming Negativity Using the *BEEP* System

TURNING UNDERSTANDING INTO ACTION

Now that you have a better understanding of negative people, a simple acronym, BEEP, will be used to help you remember specific actions you can take when dealing with Negators. The steps are summarized below.

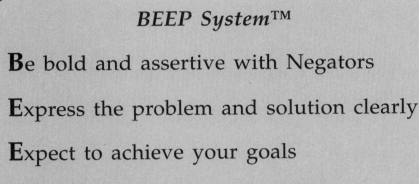

BEEP System™

Be bold and assertive with Negators

Express the problem and solution clearly

Expect to achieve your goals

Practice positive thinking

BE BOLD AND ASSERTIVE WITH NEGATORS

Remember everyone has to manage negativity in their lives. The key to success is based on how well you are able to manage it. Combining all of the information presented so far, plus the following guidelines, you will be able to be more bold and assertive with Negators (yourself or others).

► **Determine What Motivates the Individual (STEP System™)**

Keep Negators' style and likely motivators in mind when you are trying to deal with them.

► **Use the Appropriate Communication Strategy**

Once you know a Negator's style, find the most appropriate matching communication strategy.

► **Determine Their Level of Self-Esteem**

As previously explained, a person's level of self-esteem (how good they feel about themselves) is often related to being negative. The lower the level of self-esteem, the greater the tendency to feel threatened by new situations. Negators tend to react to threat by feeling angry or fearful, which further incapacitates them. When a new situation arises they feel even more threatened, angry, or fearful, increasing the likelihood of negative results. This downward cycle must be interrupted in order to turn things around.

The better Negators feel about themselves, the greater their ability to see new situations as a challenging opportunity.

► **Determine What You Can Do to Reduce Threat**

In order to help improve the other person's self-esteem and increase the likelihood of success, find out what you can do to help the Negator feel less threatened or more confident. Usually this can be determined by focusing on what is likely to be most motivating for this person (the STEP System™). The following are examples of things you can do to reduce perceived threats:

• Use "I" messages

• Keep your voice level low

- Identify past contributions

- Provide training/exposure to new technology, approaches or situations

- Listen and support

- Involve the individual in the decision-making process

- Communicate directly and often

- Be responsive to suggestions and ideas

► **Determine What You Can Do to Make the Situation More Challenging**

By focusing on high-level motivators for the individual's style, you can determine what to do to help make the new situation look like more of an opportunity to grow and develop or as a challenge to be met. A cynical/nit-picking style is more likely to be challenged if you appeal to the person's need for precision, accuracy and quality. For example, if you are introducing a new word processor and graphics software program to a secretary who is a cynic/nit-picker, emphasize the new program's ability to spell *and* grammar check, as well as the improved quality of graphics.

EXPRESS THE PROBLEM AND SOLUTION CLEARLY

It is critical to prepare your strategies in advance before confronting a negative person. To be most effective, use this two-step process.

STEP 1: Describe Behaviors and Determine Causes

STEP 2: Develop Solutions and Prepare a Script

STEP 1: Describe Behaviors and Determine Causes

When confronting a negative person or situation, start by expressing or describing the problem in clear, behavioral terms (measurable). In other words, what would you see if the situation were videotaped. Be as descriptive and factual as you can be. Examples of a poorly expressed and a well-expressed problem are illustrated in the following chart.

Problem Is Poorly Expressed	Problem is Well-Expressed
When I got to work, John was yelling and hollering like he lost his mind. He really chewed me out.	I walked into John's office at 8:30 A.M. His voice was raised and his face flushed. He said that the report he wanted from me was not ready at 8:00 A.M. and he was upset because it wasn't ready.

Note that subjective terms such as "lost his mind," "hollering" and "chewing me out" often distort the situation and tend to arouse more emotion than necessary. If in fact John took a bite out of someone, both he and the other person would be quite upset, much more so than is actually the case.

To make certain you have expressed the negative situation well, use the five Ws method for asking important questions. The first four Ws are: Who, What, When, and Where. Who was involved, what were they doing, when were they doing it, and where were they doing it?

At this early stage of asking questions make certain you do just that and avoid jumping to a solution. When you have an accurate camera-like description of the problem situation, you can proceed to ask the fifth W question (Why?) to find the cause(s).

Evaluate the Causes

The fifth W, Why?, is now involved. In order to find the underlying cause(s) of a problem with negativity, ask the question Why? until the real cause is uncovered. In the previous example, why do you believe John was upset? If we ask him "Why?" he might reply, "Because I forgot to tell you I had to have it by 8:30 A.M. and I'm really upset with myself for not giving you the correct information." Another response could have been "You never seem to listen to me." This response needs another Why? follow-up such as, "Why does that upset you?" John's response could be, "Because no one takes me seriously around here, I feel like no one appreciates me or my efforts."

The initial situation is the same, but the Why? questioning gives a more accurate picture of what is causing the problem. Obviously, the solutions to each of these problems is quite different. The use of the Why? questioning and follow-up prevents premature assumptions about a solution.

Once the underlying cause of negativity is identified, the next step is to use a systematic approach to solving the problem.

EXPRESS THE PROBLEM AND SOLUTION CLEARLY (continued)

STEP 2: Develop Solutions and Prepare a Script

The following problem-solving process provides a series of logical steps to reach a solution. Think of a situation in which negative behavior was involved. Express the situation first, and then complete the remaining steps.

► Express the problem in behavioral terms: What would it look like on videotape?

► Ask the five Ws (Who, What, When, Where, Why) to make certain you have a complete description and understand the causes. Do any research necessary to answer these questions.

Who? _____

What? _____

When? _____

Where? _____

Why? _____

► Brainstorm possible solutions and the likely results for each solution. Make a list of as many possible choices as you can.

Possible Solution	Likely Result
1. _____	_____
2. _____	_____
3. _____	_____
4. _____	_____
5. _____	_____

► Pick the best solution. Review the previous list and eliminate the solutions least likely to succeed.

► Plan how you will implement it. How will you know if you succeed?

• My plan to overcome this negative situation is to:

_____

_____

• I will know I'm successful if:

_____

_____

► Do it. Put your plan into action. Start slowly and cautiously.

► Follow-up, evaluate and modify the solution as necessary. Make any necessary modifications.

PREPARE A SCRIPT IN ADVANCE

Negative people and situations often occur unexpectedly and catch us unprepared. Have you been in a situation in which you didn't really know what to say or do at the time because you were surprised or angry? Most of us have been in that position. Sometimes after the situation has occurred you think "Darn, I wish I had said—!"

Preparing a Script

If a negative situation occurs frequently, it is important to use your experience to prepare for the next time the same or similar event occurs. You can start by envisioning the negative experience in your mind. Write down what you wish you had said. Then, think about possible alternative statements you can use in the future when this same situation occurs.

The next time (indicate the individual's name and explain the negative event)

_____ , I will say

_____ .

The individual in question is most likely to reply to my new script by saying

_____ .

My response to this will be _____

_____ .

It is important that these statements or behaviors be constructive in nature and help you feel better about yourself and the situation.

Once you have planned your script and behavior, practice using it. Some people like to close their eyes and imagine the situation in which they will use the new script. Others like to practice in front of a large mirror or role play with family or friends. You can also audio- or videotape your practice sessions to determine your effectiveness.

EXPECT TO ACHIEVE YOUR GOALS

Many people overlook the importance of setting realistic and inspiring goals. Goal-setting can motivate you to action and give you a sense of fulfillment when you achieve progress. Remember, your goals could be to overcome negative behaviors of others (Negators), as well as your own personal negativity.

The following goal assessment will help pinpoint your own strengths and areas for improvement. Before you begin, focus your perspective on your negativity goal(s): Do you wish to set a goal to overcome your own personal negativity, or do you need to set a goal to deal with one or more Negators (other people)?

Goal Achievement Assessment

Directions: Read each of the statements and rate yourself on this scale:

> 3 = frequently
> 2 = about half of the time
> 1 = occasionally
> 0 = rarely or never

_____ **1.** I think about how I will feel when I accomplish my negativity goal.

_____ **2.** When I close my eyes I can see and hear myself accomplishing this goal.

_____ **3.** I have defined my goal(s) in measurable terms (so I will know when I reach each one).

_____ **4.** I have developed an action plan to reach each one of my goals.

_____ **5.** My goals are realistic and achievable (I have reasonable expectations). I know when I will accomplish this goal.

_____ **6.** I believe that my strong efforts will have a direct impact on reaching my goals.

_____ Total Points

EXPECT TO ACHIEVE YOUR GOALS (continued)

Scoring and Interpretation

Once you have totaled the points for all six statements, you can determine your plan for future action.

17–18 Points = You are exceptional! Continue to build on your strengths.

14–16 Points = You are doing well! Improve even more by working on items rated 0 or 1.

10–13 Points = You may or may not need some improvement in this area. Focus on items rated 0 or 1.

5–9 Points = You need some improvement in this area. Focus on items rated 0 or 1.

0–4 Points = You need substantial work. Focus on all items rated 0 or 1.

Whatever your score, it is important to look at your strengths first. You can begin to acknowledge your strengths by saying—out loud—positive affirmations such as, "I am good at defining my goals in measurable terms." Repeat the positive affirmation several times before beginning to work on another area where improvement will help you achieve your goals.

Now go back and review all six statements and circle the number of any statement rated with a 0 or a 1. Both of these ratings identify areas you need to further develop. Statements #1 and #2 are important because goals are easier to accomplish when you can envision what the results feel, sound and look like. An expectation of achievement increases the likelihood of actual success.

Statements #3 and #4 are also essential for goal attainment. Being able to measure and identify when you reach a goal is just as important as having a logical plan of action to reach that goal. Set specific, realistic goals and timelines for each step of your plan (#5). Once you have developed yourself in all five of these areas, the resultant self-confidence and strong efforts can go a long way toward achieving any goal (#6).

PRACTICE POSITIVE THINKING

You can *strengthen* positive thinking by *practicing* positive thinking. In order to improve your understanding of this process, compare the mind to a radio.

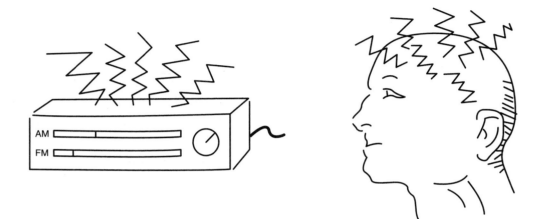

In order to hear beautiful music or lead a happy, productive life, you must first get rid of the static (negative interference). Static comes from the Negators around you, as well as the negative messages you tell yourself.

The AM/FM Approach

Tune in to a clear, positive station by using the AM/FM approach to eliminate negative static. This process is illustrated here.

► **Actual Event**

Describe the problem situation using techniques learned in this book; that is, express the problem clearly.

► **Miserable Message**

What are you actually telling yourself about the situation? In some cases your thinking has become so automatic, you may have to work backward from your current feelings to help determine the message you must be telling yourself.

PRACTICE POSITIVE THINKING (continued)

▶ **Feelings**

- *Current:* How do you feel now when this situation occurs?

- *Desired*: How would you rather feel?

▶ **Message—New**

What new script can you develop to replace the old one? Make certain the new script will result in the desired feelings. You may want to review the section on preparing a script.

An Everyday Example

This process can be better understood through the use of a common situation.

▶ **Actual Event**

While driving down the expressway you look in the rearview mirror and see a little red sports car darting in and out of traffic, cutting off other cars.

▶ **Miserable Message**

In analyzing what you are really telling yourself, you discover it is a miserable message. This message is "I can't stand it when people cut me off! If that guy cuts me off, I'm going to lose my mind!"

▶ **Feelings**

- *Current:* You feel anger, rage, upset. As a result of this thinking and feelings, your behavior is not very constructive. It involves yelling, shaking your fist and other unpleasant or negative behaviors.

- *Desired:* You want to feel calm and relaxed.

▶ **Message—New**

"I don't have to like it if someone cuts me off, but I don't have to get upset. Just slow down and let him pass me with the understanding that sooner or later the cops are going to get him."

As a result of this thinking you will no longer get upset and will cope well with this kind of driver. You will have calm and relaxed feelings.

Tune in to Your Own "Positivity"

Now it's time to apply the radio analogy AM/FM process to fine-tune your positivity thinking. Do situations occur in your life where negative static is usually present? Pick one of these situations and work through this process so you can begin getting rid of the miserable negative messages that get in the way of your success and happiness.

Personal Worksheet for Positive Thinking: AM/FM Process

Directions: Think of a situation or event that occurs repeatedly at work or home that upsets you every time it happens. Think about this situation and complete this worksheet. You may find it helpful to find the actual, unconscious miserable message you are telling yourself by asking, "What feelings am I experiencing? What must I be telling myself?"

► **Actual Event:**

_____

_____

_____

► **Miserable Message:**

_____

_____

_____

► **Feelings**

  • *Current:*

_____

_____

_____

  • *Desired:*

_____

_____

_____

► **Message—New:**

_____

_____

_____

PRACTICE POSITIVE THINKING (continued)

Practice Makes It Perfect

While this fine-tuning process may seem relatively easy, it takes practice. Even though you came up with a new constructive message that resulted in positive thinking and feelings, you have to continually and consciously repeat this "new" positive message every time this situation occurs. To continue the radio analogy, you may need to fine-tune a radio each time you turn it on unless you have a built-in electronic tuner. Your own positivity tuner can be created through self-discipline and practice.

Over the course of our lives most of us have developed a number of habitual negative messages that take place at an unconscious level. It is like riding a bike or driving a car with a stick shift. Once you learn how to do it, you no longer think about the process. When you switch to automatic, you need to think. It is like this with negative thinking.

You hear and see an event, and react to it in a predictable manner as if the event caused you to react. In reality, it is not the event itself that causes you to feel and react the way you do. It is what you tell yourself about the event that does so. In other words, your own internal messages determine how you think, feel and behave.

SECTION

V

Developing Your
Action Plan

YES!

BUILD YOUR POSITIVITY MUSCLES

To help achieve your goals for overcoming your own or others' negativity, it is important to build your mental and physical strength. Once you have prepared yourself to reach your goal(s), you need to build up your physical and mental strength for battling negativity and encouraging positivity. Positivity is the energy that comes from a healthful diet, adequate sleep, exercise, constructive stress management and meeting your own needs.

Complete the following Positivity Building Survey to find out how well you are building up your energy.

Positivity Building Survey

Directions: Read each statement and rate yourself on this scale:

> 3 = frequently
> 2 = about half of the time
> 1 = occasionally
> 0 = rarely or never

_____ **1.** I feel like I keep up with my assignments at work.

_____ **2.** I enjoy my work.

_____ **3.** I eat a healthful diet.

_____ **4.** I get enough sleep each night.

_____ **5.** I balance work with other parts of my life.

_____ **6.** I balance taking care of others' needs with meeting my own needs.

_____ **7.** I engage in regular exercise.

_____ **8.** I include humor and laughter in my life on a regular basis.

_____ Total Points

BUILD YOUR POSITIVITY MUSCLES
(continued)

Scoring and Interpretation

Once you have totaled the points for all six statements, you can determine your performance.

19–21 Points = You are exceptional! Continue to build on your strengths.

16–18 Points = You are doing well! Improve even more by working on items rated 0 or 1.

11–15 Points = You need some improvement in this area. Focus on items rated 0 or 1.

6–10 Points = You need more improvement in this area. Focus on items rated 0 or 1.

0–5 Points = You need substantial work. Focus on all items rated 0 or 1.

How well did you do? Most people practice "positivity building" in some areas and may neglect others. Set a goal to build up the specific areas where you believe you might benefit. The balance of this section provides more detail on the strategies for positivity building.

Practice the Diamond Rule

In the previous survey, if your balance is uneven between taking care of others and taking care of yourself, the Diamond Rule may become your motto: "Do unto yourself before you do unto others."

By taking care of your own needs—physical, mental, spiritual—you will build a reservoir of energy for contributing to others. Do you know what your own needs are? Are you doing something now to build up your "positivity" energy? The following personal needs assessment will help you in this process.

Personal Needs Survey

Directions: Complete the following questions.

1. What have I enjoyed doing in the past?

_____

_____

2. What do I enjoy doing now?

_____

_____

3. What kinds of work do I enjoy the most?

_____

_____

4. What kinds of social/recreational/vacation activities do I enjoy the most?

_____

_____

5. What kinds of family activities do I enjoy the most?

_____

_____

6. What kinds of spiritual activities do I enjoy the most?

_____

_____

7. If I want to indulge myself, what activities do I enjoy doing the most?

_____

_____

8. What else do I need to do more of to meet my personal needs?

_____

_____

BUILD YOUR POSITIVITY MUSCLES
(continued)

Increase Relaxation

In addition to meeting your personal needs, you can increase relaxation (reduce stress) in your life with such things as deep muscle relaxation exercises, relaxation tapes, breathing and visualization exercises, yoga, and meditation, as well as investigating various stress and time management books and courses. While this is not a book on stress management, three areas of special importance are worth mentioning:

> **Scheduling**
>
> **Experiencing Pleasant Events**
>
> **Taking Care of Your Body Through Diet and Sleep**

Scheduling

For those of you who have trouble slowing down and getting everything done, use a calendar or—better yet—an appointment book to schedule personal "positivity" building activities. Make certain you schedule the fun/recreational/social/family/spiritual activities you deem important, not just work activities and timelines.

Experiencing Pleasant Events

Recent research at the medical school of the State University of New York at Stony Brook indicates that pleasant events appear to keep the immune system stronger. In a study of 100 men, researchers found that a drop in the usual number of pleasant events more strongly predicted susceptibility to a cold than did a jump in stressful events. The researchers concluded that there appears to be a boost in the immune system from a pleasant event. The boost can persist as long as two days, while the negative effects of a stressful encounter mainly take their toll in one day. In other words, you tend to be healthier when you continue to have pleasant and fun activities and events in your life.

Plan and schedule time to do things that make you feel good. There are three activities you can engage in that cause beta-endorphins (natural chemicals) to be formed in your brain. When these chemicals are created in the brain the result is a natural state of feeling great! Research has indicated three activities cause these chemicals to be formed: exercise, laughter, and nurturance (loving or caring behaviors).

Natural Ways to Feel Good

Activity	Suggestions
Exercise	Engage in strenuous physical activity in which you sweat and your heart rate increases 20–30 minutes three times per week.
	Brisk walking, aerobics, jogging, swimming, bicycling, and some athletic activities are examples.
	Make certain you are medically capable and gradually increase time and intensity.
Laughter	Watch funny movies. Listen to or tell funny stories. Read humorous books.
Nurturance	Hug your loved ones every day. Say positive things about yourself to yourself every morning when you wake up (positive affirmations).
	Pet a loved pet.

BUILD YOUR POSITIVITY MUSCLES
(continued)

Taking Care of Your Body Through Diet and Sleep

An adequate, balanced diet and sufficient sleep help you build mental and physical strength. Avoid excessive amounts of fat and simple sugars in your diet, and make certain you eat sufficient amounts of complex carbohydrates, fruits and vegetables, and protein.

You already know how much sleep you need. Do not try to cut corners. Most of you can cut the number of hours you sleep each night for a day or two, but problems can arise if you try to do so for longer periods of time. The longer you reduce your normal sleep pattern the lower your resistance to illness. Improve your immune system for fighting all kinds of illness, as well as for fighting negativity.

Remember that the mind and the body are intertwined. You can't have a happy healthy mind and spirit without a healthy body.

APPLY YOUR KNOWLEDGE

The following is a summary overview of all techniques presented in this book. Take the opportunity to cement your knowledge by applying it now.

1. Identify a situation that appears to cause you to be negative (internal messages), or identify a Negator whom you have to deal with on a regular basis. (Remember, in individuals and situations where the primary causes are physical/medical or severely psychological in nature, the greater the difficulty in dealing with them unless other outside medical and/or psychological interventions are involved.)

_____

_____

_____

_____

2. How do you experience this negativity?

_____

_____

_____

_____

3. From the five possible causes of negativity (needs, values, attitudes, norms, and self-esteem), list what you think are the primary causes of negativity for this Negator or for yourself. Why do you believe these are the cause?

_____

_____

_____

4. Select any of the techniques in Section 2 that you feel would be helpful in confronting the negativity in question. Most of these techniques will not apply to your own negative messages, but pertain to dealing with Negators.

_____

_____

_____

_____

APPLY YOUR KNOWLEDGE (continued)

5. Identify either your behavioral style or that of the Negator (Stable, Thorough, Emotional, Pusher) and what motivates that style.

_____

_____

_____

_____

6. Write down the best communication or other strategies for dealing with the Negator in question or for dealing with your own negative messages.

_____

_____

_____

_____

7. Is the level of self-esteem below average? If so, what can be done to help increase it?

_____

_____

_____

_____

8. What, if anything, can be done to reduce perceived threat?

_____

_____

_____

_____

9. What can be done to make the situation more challenging?

_____

_____

_____

_____

10. Define the problem in measurable, behavioral terms. Make sure you use the five Ws:

What is the problem? _____

_____

Who is involved? _____

_____

When is it happening? _____

_____

Where is it happening? _____

_____

Why is it happening? _____

_____

11. Is there something that you experience repeatedly that results in your becoming quite upset? If so, what could you say or do in the future to deal more effectively with this situation? Make certain you practice it before you use it.

_____

_____

_____

_____

_____

_____

APPLY YOUR KNOWLEDGE (continued)

12. What can you do to be better prepared to reach your goals in this situation or with this person?

_____

_____

_____

_____

13. What can you do to remove obstacles that interfere with your efforts to overcome negativity?

_____

_____

_____

_____

14. Using the AM/FM process, develop a new positive message to replace the negative message you now have.

Actual Event: _____

_____

Miserable Message: _____

_____

Feelings

- _Current:_ _____

_____

- _Desired:_ _____

_____

Message—New: _____

_____

15. Brainstorm possible solutions and the likely results for each solution. Make a list of as many possible choices as you can.

	Possible Solution	Likely Results
a.	_____	_____
b.	_____	_____
c.	_____	_____
d.	_____	_____
e.	_____	_____

16. Pick the best solution(s). Review the previous list and eliminate the solutions least likely to succeed.

17. Plan how you will implement it. How will you know if you succeed?

18. My plan is to:

_____

_____

• I will know I'm successful if:

_____

_____

19. Do it. Put your plan into action. Start slowly and cautiously.

20. Follow-up, evaluate and modify the solution as necessary. Make any necessary modifications.

REFERENCES

Organizations:

American Management Association; 135 West 50th St., NY, NY 10036

Customer Service Institute; 101 Wayne Ave., Silver Springs, MD 10026

Publications:

Allesandra, Tony and Janice, and Michael O'Connor. *People Smart.* La Jolla, CA: Keynote Publishing, 1990.

Journal of Applied Psychology. Vol. 73, N.2, 193–198. 1988.

Massey, Morris. *The Mysteries of Motivation.* Minneapolis, MN: Carlson Learning Company, Inc., 1988.

Assessment Instruments:

Carlson Learning Company
1-800-686-8477

Personal Profile System®
(Provides an in-depth understanding of the behavior patterns of self and others.)

Personal Development Profile®
(Provides "people knowledge" to improve interpersonal relationships.)

Personal Profile Preview®
(Provides a shortcut to creating behavioral awareness of self and others.)

NOTES

NOTES

OVER 150 BOOKS AND 35 VIDEOS AVAILABLE IN THE 50-MINUTE SERIES

We hope you enjoyed this book. If so, we have good news for you. This title is part of the best-selling *50-MINUTE*™ *Series* of books. All *Series* books are similar in size and identical in price. Many are supported with training videos.

To order *50-MINUTE* Books and Videos or request a free catalog, contact your local distributor or Crisp Publications, Inc., 1200 Hamilton Court, Menlo Park, CA 94025. Our toll-free number is (800) 442-7477.

50-Minute Series Books and Videos Subject Areas . . .

Management
Training
Human Resources
Customer Service and Sales Training
Communications
Small Business and Financial Planning
Creativity
Personal Development
Wellness
Adult Literacy and Learning
Career, Retirement and Life Planning

Other titles available from Crisp Publications in these categories

Crisp Computer Series
The Crisp Small Business & Entrepreneurship Series
Quick Read Series
Management
Personal Development
Retirement Planning

RECEIVED
AUG 1995
Mission College
Learning Resource
Services

NOTES